Place Keepers

BRENDAN GALVIN

Place Keepers

poems

LOUISIANA STATE UNIVERSITY PRESS

BATON ROUGE

2003

Copyright © 1991, 1996, 1997, 1998, 1999, 2000, 2001, 2002, 2003
by Brendan Galvin

DESIGNER: Andrew Shurtz
TYPEFACE: Adobe Garamond
PRINTER & BINDER: Thomson-Shore, Inc.

LIBRARY OF CONGRESS CATALOGING-IN-PUBLICATION DATA:
Galvin, Brendan.
  Place keepers : poems / Brendan Galvin.
    p. cm.
  ISBN 0-8071-2891-0 (cloth : alk. paper) —
  ISBN 0-8071-2892-9 (pbk. : alk. paper)
  I. Title.
  PS3557.A44P57 2003
  811'.54—dc21

                                                  2003007304

Thanks are due the editors of the following periodicals, in which some
of the poems herein first appeared: *Crab Orchard Review, Crazyhorse,
Georgia Review, Gettysburg Review, Idaho Review, Laurel Review, Orion,
River City, Seattle Review, Shenandoah,* and *Tar River Poetry.*

CONTENTS

CONTENTS

MAY DAY

for Ellen

Suddenly tugged from behind, the work
of an oriole, one spray of the apple tree's
floweration is trembling, looking the way
it feels when a fish begins nibbling
your line. Isolations of nuthatch
and chickadee are slowly giving way, warming
into affinities. It began a month ago:
goldfinches blew into the pussywillows
and swung on the stems until we saw
that the uppermost catkins
had already sprung their bee fuzz.
Think of Catesby sketching a treefrog
clinging to the New World's
skunk cabbage, or his buffalo of the woods
engaging an itch with a bristly
locust tree: those juxtapositions,
like you and me, that prove it takes
two of anything for something to happen.

I

The old boatwright Avery Bearse is dead
again, and it's your turn
to build the skiff. A gray outport
on a stony coast, with skies the color
of wharf shacks. The tools on your list
will be coming by late bus: fishtail
gouge, bench dog, dovetail jig,
bullstone. It isn't those that get you,
but the sad-sounding ones Avery
knew by hand, froe and scarp,
fretsaw like something you might coax
a threnody with. Worse are the tools
you have no idea about, the rifflers
and eye punches, inshaves, trammel-heads.
This dream of yours is a lot like that joke
the Shingler pulled when you were a kid
and roofing the Outermost Motel: Go over
and ask Arkie Johnson can you borrow
his funk chunker. Except that you
have to get Avery Bearse to that island
on the oyster-colored edge out there,
before it wears thinner than curtain lace.
Valsay it's called, and in some places Fulva.
Another Celtic take on the world's
footlessness, last week it was spotted
off the coast of Sollay: a sudden calenture
or trick of light where the sea
should be open all the way to Canada.
And now cloud shadow creeps
across those slopes. The wind downshifts
on the road from Baffinland. You stand with
your list at what those mean laughers inside
claim is the bus stop, under a lamp
the bugs won't visit for another seven months.
Trying to find a way to deliver Avery Bearse
to the other side of cold water, all you can think
is how this life is a lot like your mother's

old lament: First they tell you
you've got the wrong screwdriver, then
they say you've got the wrong screw.

Sepias of an old winter: a man standing
full height under a berg like a grotto
deposited on the beach, behind him
the marshes a frieze of no color,
spiky with terrors, and a northwest wind
you can almost hear in the photo.

He is Herman Gill, keeper of Blue Island
Lighthouse. After months of winter,
he has logged how snowy owls
have drifted down to float criss-cross in
spook flights before the beam of his great light,
and how they refuel their yellow eyes
on the wild offspring of his children's rabbits.

All night his bachelor quarters complain
around the stove. One morning
along his beach route he came upon
a white owl untying the mysteries of a cod,
and more fish sealed in a slab of ice
nearby, like sequined slippers.

Watched by snow, he has learned to look
about him for a pair of gold eyes,
and has minted a weather saw for his logbook:
a white owl in November
means weather you'll remember.

This morning, March 14, he wrote,
Brushing soot from the cold flue ledge, I touched
a thing so soft—a finch, I saw by its beak,
with feathers now gray as a catbird's
from beating long in the chimney
it had entered to get out of the wind.

It died in a blind shiver behind the stove
as I wondered was it the same bird
that beat on the light's windows,
golden in that glare one night, wings
a transparent yellow, lost, confused,
then swept away, the glass reading
twenty-seven, the windspeed fifty-four—
so I thought of Cora and the children,
and our house flaked to a puzzle
by the Doane Brothers and barged
to the mainland for reassembly.

Here there are days so empty of speech
I believe I could detect the sound
light makes as it creaks around toward
equinox, even hear the pop
of Cora's daffodil leaves
taking their explosive stance about
the imminent flower.

But then I open the door to find
only wind bushing around the walls,
and one morning the passing
crew of the *Hannah Rich,* waving on deck
as though reprieved of mortal duty,
a joyride of breaking ice
that kept them and left for the horizon.

THE PROPER NAME FOR WATER

(a USGS map of 1940)

Given fogs mythic enough
to saw and chunk out like ice,
and ice buckling its plates so the bay
seems a frozen graveyard of Steinways,
given moon-driven tides the east wind
throws a cold shoulder into, flooding
uplands, and northeasters rumbling
nameless to whiteout, given hurricanes,
run-of-the-bay lake-effect blizzards,
and the sea forever battering entry
and outlet, what else on earth
is as worked against as these sometime
land-by-water places? You will not take
a pie-on-the-sill whiff off a breeze
from Aunt Rachel's Nook, or gain
High Cedar Island in your lifetime.
One is a cove the tide fills twice a day,
the other a quick-change sandbar,
deferred to locally as a trickster.
Though kingfishers fold away into
mudbanks here and there, and elsewhere
fiddler crabs invade on the tide lapse,
hummock, flat, gutter and slough
are where we can't remain long.
Whoever Veeney was, tonging or hauling
pots above Veeney's Hole, no one
living can say. Even Thorfinn Karlsefni,
his craft clinker-built and flexing over
the outer bar again, would find these reaches
everywhere different and the same. This chart's
cord-grass clumps only say it again:
the proper name for water is water.

Greeny gray-brown warblers this morning,
flocking through, too iffy to identify,
and gulls on the fish-house roofs
looking into it: something is up and the birds
know it. The states on our screens look flimsy.
South of here, waves are climbing each other,
out of order, anxious to come ashore
and escape that hothouse bloom,
that last lethal flower of summer, tropical yellow
and red on the tube, rootless;
where stamens and pistils should be,
a silence like a mind thirty miles wide
driving the chaos around it.

I look at these pines, wondering which
I should ask for allegiance as they bow
and flex, corkscrew and curtsy to survive,
their needles on the skylight pointing
the wind's indecisions. What lie
can I tell this garden? That the canoe
I just put away is only a peapod it might
approximate next year? It's over.
Picking the last heavily knuckled pole beans,
and the squash striped like beach umbrellas,
all I had hoped to keep thriving another month,

I remember Carol and Edna, those storms
companionably named like girls who taped
our initials to their thighs, whose tans
immortalized us, then left us soaked
inside and out, the heels of our perceptions
in the air. Tomorrow means November
two months early. Someone will swear he saw
an Adirondack chair flying back
to its mountains. The yacht *Valhalla*
leaning to starboard in Atwood Lane,
a robed court of cormorants presiding over

a thicket of lopped yardarms and masts,
the roots of things will be revealed. Shook up
and shaken out like loose change
in that bilious light, we'll see the harbor
through places we never saw the harbor before.

JOB DESCRIPTION

Most days it's like being outside
a glass telephone booth
in a strange town, the door
jammed shut and the phone
ripped out. Then, that morning
last September, for instance,
you and I take the canoe to the river
and push off, letting the current
carry us, dipping our paddles
only to hold off the banks overhung
with chokecherry, poison ivy,
wild highbush blueberry tangled
in swamp rose. We steer off
a platoon of turtles sunning
on a half-sunken log, doughboys
keeping watch across a watery
no man's land—there it begins,
the stepping back from the literal.

Above an island of cord grass,
sudden hundreds, bank swallows
lifting together and warping over us
like a rush of wind we have never
heard before, and later, one cormorant
on a dead snag hanging out its wings
to dry: insignia, Austro-Hungarian,
and I see that whoever invented
the vampire wasn't looking at bats.

Home at this desk a year later
or the next day, it can feel like setting
a foot on that river and finding it
buoyed up, then the next step
supported, and the third. Boat, water,
bird, again these unwilled choices
from the odd, strewn lumber of
consciousness. Every time

my paddle stirs a swirl I can hear
between these lines the Segovia
you've put on, and among tangled
shoreplants, your dishwasher's
bump and grind. My lady,
the uncommon music of your house.

1. A quick flurry of snow buntings
    flocking here and there above
    the dunes and marsh grass,
    and remnant sanderlings, brant,
    horned larks, such spectacle
    I would have tripped over that
    thing spotted like the wrack line
    had I not heard it crooning
    to itself and seen the flipper
    wave as though it was orating
    or working out whether
    to slough a skin and walk into town,
    giving someone seven years of joy
    before a lifetime of trouble
    and a patrimony for the books.
    Hauled out on the beach
    it might have been any sun lover
    waiting on its back for July,
    off guard and unaware because
    nobody's standing here in the wind
    these bottom months, only me.
    It raised a face round-eyed
    and whiskered, a cartoon uncle's
    caught in the act, though the retreat
    into its element was almost casual,
    a slow-motion sack race.
    Then those eyes were drawn
    to shrewdness under heavy brows,
    the skull a helmet, olive drab—
    one of the seal folk was studying
    a man hauled out of his routine
    and relating some grievance to the sea.

2. *The Bones*   They are brown here in the lee
of Gull Island, like old wood
carved and sanded.
                          The tide
that visits them strips away veneer
so they look shipped across time
as well as water,
                          and yet I want to say
I knew the harbor seal whose flesh
contained them as its instrument.

Last winter there were times
it fled the riverbank, a shadow
in the current, then a face

breaking from the flow, as eye to eye
we checked each other out.

Eyes are the first to go in the lee
of Gull Island, and then the face. Fallen
things are not long in the flesh here,

but this has left a harp or lute,
medieval, to fit between a hand
and clavicle, or balance on a knee.

It has a neck, a fingerboard and frets—
a forty-stringed sarangi, perhaps,
unstrung now, or else a koto or tarab,

tuned with these pegs and keys,
something a bow or plectrum
drew music from, which now is elegy.

Maybe you escaped from the marsh
when that heron began scarfing
all it could into its gaping rictus,
lining blue skin and bones
against what was coming. You were
no stone ornament on those rocks
around the garden pool, slickskin,
rubberhead, and we loved your virid
look of a critic assessed for back taxes.
There were signs and portents enough:
in those days with yellow-rumped
warblers fugitive in their margins,
we brought in the fantails
and black mollies. Fieldmice began
shifting their bones and slipping
their envelopes of skin into the shed
behind your pool, strewing turds
delicate as lettuce seeds, balling up
nests in our Santa stuff. One night
in Ellen's sleep a Canada goose
swam in the pool, eating the water hyacinths
and bamboo. Told to scram, "Can we talk?"
it inquired, then climbed into
a lawnchair that collapsed with the dream.
What else to say about you? Aesop
would have known. Maybe something about
understanding when to make the leap?
On Twelfth Night you said nothing.
After the Snow Moon, owls brought their
lovenotes around; ice on the pool
released you, eyes buttoned tight,
your tongue giving my sympathies
the year's first raspberry.

All night the wind locomotive in the eaves,
and this morning an industrial glassworks
on tree limbs and wires.
                            Still, I keep thinking
of the river, its blue mussels clinging
by their beards to the rocks, sun touching
even the grayed-out cedar shakes

on wharf shacks, an afternoon when
it will be barely April for a couple of hours,
with me walking the subtidal mud, hammer
and burlap bag in hand
                            while the river's departed
for its conference with the bay, leaving only
a few shallow pools as rearguard.

Those mussels will be thriving
sweet and fat with glycogen
and a long winter's blossoming plankton then.

Outside, dunelands are on the move,
white, tidal, with spume and banners
blowing off the drifts.
                            In the ice glaze
a pitch pine, keeling over on a wire,
or down the line a substation blowing,

and by candlelight, the woodstove
is thrumming and flaring like an engine room,
and I cast forward a month or two, remembering how

those mussels are nowhere as elegant
as their cousins the littlenecks, and unlike
their cousins the oysters are never mistaken
for aphrodisiacs,
                            but to shellfish who've survived
green crabs and red tides, hydroids, and larval

aliens released with the ballast water of ships,
such distinctions are nothing.

Each of them has a heart, and filters
twenty gallons of river every day, finding therein
more than a billion nutritious tidebits.

Who says we don't admire what we can't
understand? Not even when they're cleaned up,
given a G.I. shower with a stiff brush?

Not even steamed in a good ale with
chopped garlic, andouille, and a few other
diced and sprinkled mysteries?

Questions I'll ask the sleet flung in my face
like thumbtacks on my way
to the woodpile and all the way back.

Slipping around the bend
of an instant, a shy,
wingèd thing, a spindleshanks
for hanging a body on,
if the soul can be seen

when it takes on the color of river ice
or a wall of reeds, shapes itself
to a cedar, then to a place where bark
sloughed off a gray pine trunk,

and the river's never the same
river twice, but a mirror to the eagle's
passing rumor and the now-and-then
of geese jockeying down the air
to announce opening water,

then the soul is the river's constancy,
and you are the soul of the river,
great blue, always near,
even on this winter morning—a lobe
of southern air pushing in until it's April
or October for a few hours again—

ice on the river going, the last
snow under roadside
bittersweet and chokecherry
like edges of seafoam,
the marsh hawk up and hunting,

heron, and you've been hunting, too,
your wet footprints crossing the road,
three toes and a spur, like a line
of tree runes on the asphalt, until that wind
chopping up the bay arrives to erase them.

2

How often have we had coffee that tastes of window,
bread that tastes of corner, cherries that taste of kiss?
—GABRIEL GARCÍA MÁRQUEZ

There are mornings your brown oatmeal bread
tastes like the road to Ballyconeely,
I swear, with random magpies leaping
out of the ditches across our windshield.
What mix of ingredients under
your hands sets this off? McCann's
whole Irish oatmeal, stone ground
wheat flour, buttermilk? This morning
I'm tasting Sweeney's Hotel in Donegal.
Here come those sainted ladies
out of the kitchen, bearing wild salmon
on platters wide as their smiles,
lamb noisettes in mint butter sauce,
steak and oyster pies, colcannon and stelk,
new peas, carrots and greens—except
this is breakfast right here in America,
I'll hold onto that, and brown, nutty Irish bread,
viaticum for the wayfarer. Down in my belly
I can feel it fitting me for communion
with unpronounceable saints
who hang their cloaks on shafts of sun
and sleep in hollow trees. The next year
Sweeney's Hotel wasn't there, only bog,
another island of hospitality that comes
and goes in those mists rich as buttermilk.
But now I'm gazing at windless water
the evening's draining down, with the tide
that's slipping between silhouetted
islands, an effect of oatmeal Dr. Johnson
knew nothing about. Tell me you see it too,
this place where history put in for blood
and left mist ghosting. It's breakfast—America,
I know, not Bealaclugga or Rosbeg. Why
peat smoke then, like a whiff of burning tire?

Why sheep and silence, with a few shorebirds
piping, and a single house, its whitewash reflecting
on that water? If it's seven a.m. in America,
why are we pushing in through this door?

(Outer Hebrides)

He's a wee handy man, climbing
onto the bumper to whack the battery
into compliance with a stillson.
Now the little green bus turns over and begins
to lurch forward, and he settles it
into fifteen miles an hour. "A quarter
of a million on her," he says,
"and good for another." It's him and me,
and I'm here for the *machair,*
twenty miles of buttercups, orchids, vetch
and birdsfoot trefoil exuding a yellow haze
that floats just above the ground
the whole western length of the island,
the Atlantic beyond through lapses of dune.
Greenshank country, with snipe signing
the air in random whistling zig-zags,
lapwings, redshanks, oystercatchers,
and the ruins of a second-century
wheelhouse at Kilphedar. He's here
because somebody in Ulster an eon ago
got tired of dodging Niall of the Nine Hostages
or his like, and rowed over one night
to discover fishing and farming
were more congenial to a long life.
One eye's on the road, one's studying
my rucksack and seventeen-pocket parka,
and he's no doubt wondering why anyone
would go into the *machair* except
to pasture cows. "Have a care if you get
up island, " he says. "The army may be
banging about on their missile range
today. Ach, I've sailed merchant marine
around the world, and they hate
the English everywhere." He'll stop
for anyone who can raise a hand,
at Howmore, by the corner of the road

to Ormaclete, near a house
glued all over with starbursts
of purple mussels and scallop shells,
"I'll be along" his only schedule.
They're old women mostly, heading off
for lochside houses, and one ancient couple,
joined by the handles of a plastic grocery bag,
all of them speaking "the Garlic,"
weather talk I'm guessing. "A hen harrier!"
I must have just shouted it, because I'm
the one pointing. And I'm the foolish one
when he wrestles the steering wheel
and pulls the bus over so I can take in
the silver male hawk circling the bog
and they can take me in, all of them smiling,
pleased I've come all the way from America
to admire their island, or else this
is how they handle the mad. The bird
sails off east toward the mountains.
"Thank you," I say to no one
and everyone, and back on the road
they're smiling and nodding at me,
speaking that poetry of conspirators,
and our driver says, "One of us
wants to know where a man
might buy a pair of boots like those."

STILLBORN

Well into the nineteenth century, in parts
of the Outer Hebrides, a stillborn infant
was buried in a remote place among
the rocks reserved for that purpose.

I fell nameless out of time and was
brought to the mountain by strangers,
my father's friends, before
I could be handed sunwise around
the ring of my sisters and brothers
rhyming their wishes for me. Now
I am daughter of rock, whose breath
entered this stone before the midwife
could pour from the cup of her palm
a droplet to fill me with graces,
another to prompt charity in my voice,
and a third for my pluck against
the gnome of the rocks. My father
leans to the plow, turning the fields
in his accustomed clothes, as he did
on my first and last day, under pain
of a childless future should he fall
to the grief he sows in those furrows.
Rain within wind, sun within rain,
my mother grinds at her quern,
her heart salting each handful of meal.
Though I have seen the wee host
riding astride the ragwort over the water
from Uist to Barra, from Barra
to Mingulay, O human people,
even your sorrow is finer than anything
I have. Gathering dulse, hitched into
the circle of tilling and harvest,
collecting eggs of the sulaire,
you let that world escape your esteem
as a wave escapes rock. Nothing here
compares with only an oystercatcher

flying above summer. Quick as the smell
of oatmeal on that hearth, cries
from its orange beak pass through me.

Some mornings, missing the feel of lather
and the blade, one of those Ballyloskey farmers
creeps into my mirror for a second,
face like a woodknot with blue eyes.
Sometimes in wind I can almost
hear them rooting for me, all the dead
from Ballyloskey, point of origin:
eternity as spectator sport.
That human compost pushed me out
into this vale of duffers and fumblers,
and may one day take me back, but for now
they watch the moves of everybody
they've passed their looks and lights to,
making the side bets and the accusations:
He got that attitude from you folk. And why
shouldn't the dead enjoy us? It's more fun
than harping on forever, a lot less dangerous
than Valhalla. Today they may be saying,
He's only scratching with a pen. Let's see
what his cousin the police chief is up to.
Sometimes a flash off a store window
gives me a few faces in passing, ditch-beards,
pie-eyed color commentators, a lineup
of root vegetables, nobody too far
off the ground. Behind them the mountain
is laced with stone walls, there's a celtic cross
or two, and hard by a jar of plastic flowers,
a jug of the right stuff, then the whole
graveyard swept with cloud.

EPIPHANY

"As kingfishers catch fire . . ."

The deep groaning of red horsepower,
colored lights strobing up Elm Street,
and suddenly I am ten and famous

because my grandfather's barn loft
down at the end of the last wild patch of field
the triple-deckers have cornered
is putting forth smoky tendrils.

It's my grandfather's barn,
a leftover pastoral where he kept a horse
and grew vegetables
                          out of an inclination
or necessity he brought over the water
from Inishowen and took with him
out of the world as fire now is taking
his barn out of the world.

But spontaneous combustion—
who knew that without playing with matches,
or big kids smoking,
                          flames could simply
appear, danger so dire no one spoke of it?

My grandfather's barn, and suddenly
I am everywhere,
                          don't know how
to stand still until a fireman huge
and alien as a Roman legionnaire lifts me
into his face,
                          "Get on that sidewalk
and stay there," putting me back on earth.

Fifty years now an anonymous sky-blue ranch
has sat where the barn's thick stanchions
supported the dark
              and we slammed grounders
at each other and buttonhooked for passes
among the burrs and stickers,
                    and I am left with
a first phrase catching fire: spontaneous combustion,
like inscape, epiphany, like love at first sight.

Once it took the field
we forgot its ripsaw profile
and the tail barely a rope fray,
no rudder, and the whole
satchel-with-legs look of it
alongside the Sampsons
and Delilahs of the breed.
Locked in its work trance,
mind over sheep-fuddle,
streaking out low it collected
and bullied them as though
they were stray thoughts
of the shepherd who stood,
cap over brow, canny,
whistling his dog through all
the right moves: when
to charge, lie low, display
just the exact hint of threat
to back that big ewe down,
then go neat-footed, closing
the distance, adjusting
the angle, black-and-white
verb to the flock's blackfooted
milling. How long after these canids
willingly approached our fires
did it take for some magus
to train one up to these workaday
marathons, this serious play
that involves everything from
pick-up-sticks to a log-roller's
quickstep over the backs
of Charolais built like a herd
of tractors? Now it has queued
the flock up at the second gate,
walked them through it and home

again to that foxy whistler
who's swapped his Wellingtons
for soft Italian loafers today.
The dog cuts two out of the flock,
melds them in again, heads them
toward the pen while a beauty
without vanity shimmers unaware
of itself over the rough field,
shivers the spine as—applause
like a smattering of stock doves
flying—the white gate closes.

Nightly now, under the Snow Moon,
they are singing of Love as they understand it—
that big-ticket item that leaves us tongue-tied.
So their offspring will land with roof-thumps
over our heads, come next May, they sing it
as they were meant to, *basso profundo*
in moonwhite that magnifies leaf scutter,

for no reason at all recalling how,
in Dingle once, I stepped from a phone booth
into a swirl of long-stemmed bridesmaids
debouching from cars—O attar of petals,
dangerous pastels—and, shrunk to crocus height,
I was willing to be that tall forever.

So what if some critical strain of eighteen-wheeler
rips through these moments? That's what I asked the dark
last night when the owls woke me. So what if it happens
between that memory of bridesmaids and this one
of owls courting? Those old Greeks had it wrong:

to never have been at all, that would be worst,
to have missed these moments that arrived
unbidden merely because we were here,
never to have woven a lifetime of these
momentary joys into a life—

my dog Finnbarr, asleep on the deck one morning
while a nest-making titmouse plucked hairs from his back,
woke up and turned to the sun, unsurprised,
giving the bird more time to complete its moustache.

Or that moon out the kitchen window, a licorice wafer
fallen from the roll. Until, along its southeastern edge,
a thread of light began, never before in sixty years, maybe
never again, backlit with the silence of October dawn.

3

You sat on the white line
at a bend of Long Pond Road,
if you are who I think you were,
and posed for a snapshot,
daring the lack of traffic
in rolled jeans and saddle shoes,

legs crossed, with a fan of hair
your scarf almost tamed,
back when I hoped *forever*
would pass by high-school osmosis
from my palm into yours.

Whoever you are now, three carts ahead
in the checkout line, I make it
eighteen thousand days
since your face reflected firelight
at Fisher's Beach. Time hasn't softened
everyone in such a generous way.

Your purchases ring up
sensible and spare: children must be
grown and gone, but above
your checkbook and gold ring
that slight puzzlement's still there.

Tell me I'm not so far gone
that if I leaned into your purview
I couldn't bring back the way pine trunks
lay down their shadows, barring the light
with purples across sandy roads,

back when excitement was the sun
oxidizing Nemasket Cola signs
and a deer fleeing us up ahead,
freezing my scalp, was at first
a doberman, every time.

Old Bob Gray coming sudden
around a bend was another bristling moment,
underlined by the locust's buzz,
the town's senior collector of silences,
in high summer his sweat-salted hat
full of blueberries the size of dimes.

Behind rimless glasses, his movie-lifer
face and his bare nod in passing
kept us going toward a skinny-dip pond
with pickerel schooled in its shallows,
plier-mouthed, chained, like hardware
in the flesh,
                 or a heron crossed
so high above us the sun made
transparencies of its wings. Certain
that Bob Gray watched from the trees,
you'd dive through my hands like silk anyway.

Those blue, living, unbroken acres
breathed the underleaf cool of the day
back into the dusk, and whippoorwills,
nightly, were still possible, but
figment or fragment of fifty years ago,
you are gone through the glass doors
into that dark again, memory's
glory hole, where the light in your eye
like a hypnotist's watch
is spinning in my own.

Take that snapping turtle we found
in the third of the chain of ponds
last Thursday, its shell bossed and lugged
like a rusted wheel thrown in
among the arum and duckweed,

so short-tempered it flourished its stone
fist-axe of a head against the approach
of our canoe, more crocodile than blacksnake,

and three days later, beside our path,
the endangered ladyslipper, a benign maze
that coats the bee's fur with pollen
before it can escape to trap itself again
in another pink scrotal sac—

all spring we'd looked for it on our rambles,
only to find it underfoot in one of those niches
where the towhee kicks litter around,
thriving on neglect, where you get
what you wouldn't think to search for:

alongside the useless, the randomly beautiful;
things banned with things protected;
the glandular-hairy by the toothed and spiny.

Take that thistle guarding our door last September,
armed and dangerous, its cultivation
outlawed in thirty-seven states, and call it
a gallowglass for hire to no one but its own
stickle-backed containment,

and call that ladyslipper by one of its other names:
mocassin flower, whippoorwill's shoe,
or even camel's foot, since it's that rare,

and imagine a reptile so old and other-worldly
it laid eyes on a man who stayed a night
in that white house by its pond,
but can't remember and wouldn't care
that his name was Thoreau.

Kiln-dried Andalusian maple, blonde walnut,
and the other nonexistent hardwoods,
and the fabrics of Utopia: Cambrelle,
Modacryl, Primaloft, Krylon—
it isn't the stuff they're made of
that we want, but this whole room,
the order in it and what isn't: us.

We want the room just before we enter
with that denning-animal fetor we detect
in our own rooms when something
between a bear and a Marx Brother
seems imminent, when at night our odd-lot
furniture bristles, jostling for space.

We all want to be durable
and retain our lustrous sheen
like these catalog rooms
that shelter the desk where no one
has lost our file yet, and the table
across which the irretrievable word
hasn't been thrown,

rooms that would change us
if only we didn't enter dragging
that father before grandfather
beyond forebear who walks around
in us furcapped and bushy, reeking
of bogwash, spill and splat.

You might have made something
to capture those hand-me-down
gewgaws and clunky chains
you used to drape on yourself
like a little Houdini of trumpery
whenever you played grownup.

Instead you remembered
how I swear I can hear kitchen machines
grinding late at night over
which one's turn it is
to break down this time,
and how they know it whenever I get
five dollars ahead of them.

Maybe you could see the way
my head tightened
like an old peanut butter jar
full of the bolts and nails
I need most when the cap's
locked in rust.

This morning, as you listened
to a soccer talk show on that far island,
studying the patois before
you interview its finance minister,
I opened the closet door on the toolbox
you made in shop—hinged,
painted red, with a wooden
handle you sanded and shellacked
all by yourself, with a snap lock
and fitted lift-out tray.

In the house beautiful
of the ideal, we won't need
to arrest the drift of pliers
and screwdrivers from room
to room. We won't need tools
or fresh red paint at all.

But today, remembering
when you hopped off the schoolbus
and came swinging something
pridefully up the driveway,
a daughter like you and a red toolbox,
I know why sometimes the world
needs to be flawless imperfectly.

Not you again, they might be thinking,
and roll their eyes, look shyly
down into the water troughs, hoping
I'll go away. The drivers, too,
beery and unimprovable as ever,
sitting like Fat Tuesday on their
theatrical barouches, study me
as though I'm from Free the Mules:
no raunchy come-ons, never an offer
to take me anywhere. Under the insults
of straw farmer hats or a headpiece
like an over-the-hill Rockette's,
the mules still bear dignity up
like a halo supported by the alertness
of their ears. I come here because
that first time I saw them, framed in
wrought iron a moment,
far from cotton and red clay, saw
where the traces had worn their flanks
to shiny patches like a Good Will sofa,
I admired their reserve before the heavy
tour of embarrassments with cameras,
and wondered why they haven't revolted
against the conspiracy on anything
that shows a spine in this life.
But they don't, and there's more
than endurance here. Whatever it is,
that obstinacy mixed with something else,
it stops me cold among the confusions
of the Quarter, and draws me down here
by the river and the old French Market.

Last fall I drew a wild pre-music
of squeaks and cries from those knots
of oak and maple, and unlocked
a few rounds to those charred places
where lightning entered the standing tree
and paused, flickering around as if
lost, then went on through the roots.

This morning there was a bivouac
of old leaves stuffed in among the cords,
and a gray tangle of fieldmice
that moved off white-handed with their fear
into the woods, recalling the Book of Kells
for me: St. Matthew's gospel, foot of
the first page, between the Chi and Rho—

there two mice are in a tug-of-war
over a piece of bread, and behind each a cat
is ridden by another mouse rooting
them on. Such holy wit was possible
beyond the pale of Rome, a scribe
escaping his crammed lines of majuscule
just long enough to illustrate some theory:

—That there will always be more rodents
than their nemeses?—That when it comes
to games the cats and mice are in cahoots?
—That since the latter ride the former,
the mice are in control as long as
they maintain their variant Scheherazade
defense and entertain their keepers?

That was this morning, but now all theories
are off. The baby two-foot redtailed
hawk who stops traffic by standing
in the road and shrieking panic hunger
of the newly fledged, unslakable pure fact,
is waiting on my woodpile in silence.

I have sat for hours in a corner
where my chalk and two blackboards
met but failed to comply with cursive charts
above them, the future closed to me

a foot away, the world sliding downhill
because I didn't know what put me
in that chair where Washington
looked down above Miss Dillingham,
white-haired both, in dowager's
throat lace, their lips pressed in a line

as if to say, *Be serious like us
and even you may rise into a frame
up here, or grace a dollar.*

And because I have stood for seasons
on the corner of Ferry and Broadway,
where two drunks argued over whose
dog was smarter and *The Treasure
of the Sierra Madre* showed
at the Rialto for the eleventh year,

my hair combed into wings that weren't
getting me anywhere until Victor Russo,
mistaken for his cousin Victor Russo,

got shot, I've earned this corner of my garden
where the emperor pole beans build their
rain forest a little higher every day and sail
their blossoms like red tropical birds above it,

and real hummingbirds patrol, spooling
vertically before my eyes, checking me out
while I celebrate their rude good health and how
these beans make such efficient use of rain.

There's a new complication in
that spraddle of branches just beyond
the pines, not fifty feet from this window
where I'm working a reluctant poem:
a deer, like shadow on snow, then two,
picking their way, nibbling cedar
and scrub ten feet from the clothesline.
Fifteen degrees, windless, a three-day
storm coming and they know it;
even I do, seeing a slate-colored
junco turning indigo, and four
deer now, daring a silence
that grows after the schoolbus
whines on through, a yellow rebuke
to this page where the poem came
close enough to show me a face
ruminating a mouthful of juniper.

Tonight, being old enough, I can smile
in the dark, hearing the little plumbers
prying up the floors of a house
within this house, this place not home,
its radiators stamped 1913. Do they ever
knock off for the day, or take a coffee break?
I picture them in caps and coveralls
from a childhood story, banging around
all night in the pipes and coils
with miniature stillsons, and recall
the little people in my grandmother's village,
bringing luck to all who welcomed them
without questioning their manners.
Since their smithy is at it all hours,
who did that alarm clock rouse,
trilling across the other afternoon?
And yesterday, though it wasn't Sunday,
I listened at a valve while churchbells
summoned them as if to a steeple
under Tinker Mountain. How far have I come
from the knee of white-haired Mary Barr
if, hearing the rain discoursing along gutters
in that world within this world,
and the sky in a radiator
unleashing its full complement of starlings,
I admire how the old gods always
find a way from under whatever hill
they were banished to?

We are in over your head.
Explain our night moves
as a few leaves trying
for braille on a wall,
but I and my kind are
between you and the day,
inhabiting spaces you own
but have never seen.

Inquisitive to a fault,
though never acquisitive,
goblets, copper-bottom pots,
pond ripples caught and held
in well-grained cabinetry,
all the appointments of
your life are our debris.

Free your house's waters,
retract its light, and when stars
over the rooftree drip cold,
our brainy hands remember
the way to the old denning place,

ours before you strained
oceanic light through such tall glass
and made pasta by hand,
before the Algonquians
named us *arahkunem.*

Night stirs its branches,
but in time we're a smell
you cut after through our floor
and we see you down there.
Our young huddle in a corner,
but a few of us pad over
and look in on you,
bystanders at a construction site.

4

These are the faces we made down there
to entertain each other. We were green,
marble-sized, scabbed over and rutted
when you threw us into the compost
last fall. After nights of rain that swelled
and softened the earth so we wondered
how any of you anywhere ever thought
it was flat, we returned from exile
and you shoveled us under the rototiller
to be rendered impossible. Fiddleheads
down in the marsh arose from their own
torn parchment and mummy cloth,
and we shoved up, thick-stemmed among
the early unfurlings of squash and beans,
and in evenings of broken thrush music
began drawing gold-centered,
lavender starbursts out of ourselves,
in concert with the sleeping trees:
red dwarfs in the maples, constellated
petals of wild apple. We had toughened up
in that rejects' underworld the chickweed
flourished over. Now you have drawn us
into September, volunteers caught out
in our proletarian jackets, but don't
misread us. Whether as slave food
or aphrodisiac, we have always been
in politics, and though never educated
like the artichoke, or fopped-up
like certain squashes, we can be multiplied
by anyone, prepared more ways than bread.
You are tired of living when you're tired of us.

Now from this island of deadfall
at the road's bend, the sudden
conflagration of an oriole's song.
What music in there among
the wind-broken and upstanding
pines and oaks, poplars
sprung through jagged breaks,
what nestings after the overtures
and proposals emanating from five kinds
of bird-berry coverts, roses, catbrier
and fiddlehead tangles.

These thickets make a weir
for trapping wind-traveled seeds,
and on this May morning a shoal
off the flyway's northward flow.
Out of such places a double handful
of pine duff and ancient leaves
may leap every ten years or so
if you're lucky, its wings whistling,
or else you may see it at roadside
of an evening, solitary, bird for
the corner of the eye: woodcock:
never walking or running,
but perambulating
as though to some crepuscular rhumba.

Or you'll listen, hair freezing on the instant,
as it climbs the mid-March twilight,
its courting music like
ice water dripping, but sweeter,
faster, and after the breakout
you may even find the shells in there,
heavily freckled, fragments
on a litter of sticks and leaves.

For themselves and their place keepers,
these tangles generate a binding
abundance, and for this morning's
oriole music that's embodied
in the bird's char and fire,
then echoed in a redstart male's
lesser black and orange in there,
the goldfinch flareups,
magnolia and Canada warblers
splashing firelight and shadow
on the leaf-turning shade
until you'd think the heat of all those
avian propositions would reduce
these thickets to their smoking roots.

This little whiff of oil paint
means someone across the fields
is at her easel again, working
in purple, it smells like,

a jar of sickle asters, or loosestrife
from down in the marsh, where sometimes
a heron will send up its head
for a periscope look around.

This next is somebody lighting up,
Macanudo, I'd say,
dark wrapper, the strength
of determination upon the day.

When fog's this thick with clues
chances are it's a cover for things
that have to happen: a hillside
releases its goldenrod:

cucumbers traveling on their useful springs
find they have crawled in with
the pole beans, imagining
who knows what hybrids, what wild repasts.

A rain of acorns woke us
to another summer slept away.
On stumps and treefall
we arose, irruptions
as dark-minded as yours,

or else a punkwood
rigadoon, or lowfalutin'
parliament: old men of
the woods; sad why-men
in a conclave under
medieval hats; sitwells;

satchels and sacheverells.
Look here: this cup and flask,
jellies, an orange peel,
oysters and a strew of lemons
sliced, a chocolate cone,

or else, depending on your view,
a ground like Spotsylvania
after the artillery rolled away,
or a wild haberdashery: cloche
and sombrero, turbans, wimples.

We blush and pale,
like you. Like you we are
mostly water, and live upon
decay. Autumn Coletti,
is that one of us, or the girl
you loved in seventh grade?

If, in our names, you find
a cast, Slippery Jack,
the rogue; Grisette, the little
match girl; the vamp False
Chanterelle; Silky Volvaria,
the racetrack tout,

even the foreign airline Fly
Agaric, too many characters
will break your story down, and we
break down: this brief prime
is our beauty, too soon
we deliquesce upon ourselves—

No rose without manure,
as you might say. Come here
at midnight and a few of us
will glow for you. On Mars
we would have been
the debutantes.

were apples, horses, and giving apples
   to horses, and floating bareback
on a Percheron named Gabe—wide as

a parlor rug and slow as a summer
   Sunday afternoon cloud—up the Stone
Arabia Road, through Illyrium Center,

Limekiln, Hammett, Starkville, some Sundays
   even as far as Bremen Lake before he'd
turn Gabe homeward. Better to check on

a couple of early ripeners than snore
   good daylight away, he'd tell you,
an after-dinner belly like a stone

dropping you through every level of sleep.
   He could see past the Aggie pamphlets,
and by its long, upright stem and yellow flesh

he knew a Sweet June that survived the notice
   of the horticultural boys behind a barn
silvered with abandonment, its loft

a purple martin lodge, the house
   out front a settlement of dust. Fruit yellowish,
under the middle size (politely put), sweet

and rich, though not an ideal keeper—this
   Thacher wrote in 1822, and as an afterthought:
chief apple of the Plymouth colony.

Sweet-June, sweet-sweet-June, Charlie Fox
   could even hear an apple-colored goldfinch
singing in the name, singing from the tree

to tell the name to whoever it was had stood
    three hundred miles, three hundred years
behind him by that bay, admiring the grandsire

of this tree. So Gabe could take his pick, Charlie
    stepped him right up to the branches—the martins
sweeping in and out the barn, blue-green as stars

across the afternoon—and thought, *A country that's*
    lost track of its apples is headed off to hell on a handcar,
then balanced on Gabe's back to fill his pockets.

Charlie Fox will look up from oatmeal
and coffee at six this morning
and see the only waterthrush all year
bobbing at the seed table out his window,
and that will be my first sign. All night
after yesterday's rain I have turned the wind
out of the northwest toward Charlie's
whereabouts, and seeded it with birds
so this afternoon a house wren
will follow his tomcat home, buzzing
like a joke tied to its tail, my second sign.

A cool night in August like this one
and the flesh of Holland Pippins and Reinettes
begins to surge. I can feel the orchard
shake as though each tree's being shivered
by a bear stocking up for a long sleep.
This morning a line of drizzle will hang
its dismal laundry above Charlie's meadow,
way down where that red buck like an early
leaf-change raises its eight-point rack
out of grass, wet muzzle working.

That's another sign I've sent him,
with the inchling toad he'll stoop for,
crossing the yard. He'll keep his fist closed,
as on a stone, warming it until it nuzzles
his palm, then Charlie will let it leap
for the congregation of morning glories.

He'll be sharpening the cutter bar by some old
corner of Queen Anne's lace and goldenrod
one of these cider-lit afternoons,
and I'll swing the breeze for censer and stop him
cold: apple musk, aroma, tang? Standing there
with his nose going at the air like a beagle's,
he'll have no adequate word for the mystery
that stuns him yearly. It's unfair, I know.
Charlie Fox might have been the Midas
of corn or alfalfa, but it matters what a man
loves, and one day he bit into
a Kittagaskee Wonder and there I was.

There's nothing more to be said, except,
one of these nights, Orion will throw
a frost-brilliant leg over the dunes again,

and we'll hear the rote of surf once more,
the peninsula beginning to breathe free
of sunblock and outlandish dreams.

By the time that star-man returns
in silence from wading the salt oceans,
every loud talker in the post office,

even those joggers with ears
electronically bunged against birdsong
on Corn Hill Road,
                                            will be dragged
back under the weight of ambition
that presses down on cities,

and all these summer supplement
artists will be gone, their reputations
faded like heat ripples at the town line.

Then we'll be the only light keepers
on our square mile of the planet. Delicious
to think of it, and of taking the long way

to Ciro's again for *zuppa, calamari,*
scampi, no need for reservations when
Orion climbs farther away from the bleeping

inane, the blather of honchos inventing
themselves on cell phones. Starlight. Silence.
Our thirty-five years under winter stars together.

Maybe the conflagration is touched off each year
when the first matchhead of a crocus flares,
which no one ever sees, but here in the planter
on the railing is a white-throated sparrow,

looking ragged as something a chef
just threw in a rage at an exhaust fan,
a peabody bird bathing in icemelt,
sending its golden droplets up as though
seeding the sunlight, not a crocus yet in sight.

So this is the source of those controlled
burns of forsythia by our houses
two weeks in April, lanterns in the drawn-out
noirs of fog, lights private as ships at sea, whereby
the mailman navigates from house to house.

A long time before we'll hear
Old Sam Peabody, Peabody, Peabody,
but immersed in total pleasure for at least
five minutes now, splashing itself, feet sunk
in the planter's mud, this bird knows the water

will freeze again, and maybe that everything
coming after—even lilacs, and shadbush ghosting
among unlit trees—depends on these yellows
it's flipping into being with its wings.

For bracts and mayapples, for a goldfinch
knocking at a window's conundrum,
this white-throat's whipping up the sunlit modulations,
sulfur, citrines, gilt, canary, amber,

for pollen, and month to month across monotonous greens,
for the wings of fritillaries thinner than onionskin,
until seaside goldenrod gathers and concentrates
saffron, packing it in for cold storage.

As for me, I'm going to keep shoving these fists
full of sickle asters in your face. Especially
when your car's broken down at roadside
and you're quaking because you don't know
what's waiting for you beyond the asphalt.
When you dread the appearance of ants
in your kitchen, I'm going to describe how
they percolate out of cupboards, that's the word,
then tell you more about apples
than you ever wanted to know: how that core
you tossed from your passing car
sprung a tree no thicker than a surf-casting rod,
which supports this booty that's weighing
my pockets down. Go ahead, walk away, close
your ears and vote with your feet. Nothing
I can tell you will fatten your checking account,
and there's nothing here to lionize. There's only
unpretending life, present and accounted for,
the cerulean warbler's brittle stance a moment
on the railing, intrepid for the run to Ecuador.
Which refutes all slaves of theory and returns them
to their gestures. Remember the morning
that black-tailed godwit from Eurasia probed the mud
between the salt pond and a sandspit the color
of its neck? That was me behind you
whispering how—separate and together, absorbed
and linked into other forms, laid in new knots
of protein, entered without will in xylem
and panicle—we might draw a wondering crowd
like us into another moment like that one.
It wasn't to frighten you, but to speak
of fecundity, as even this inchworm knows,
who lives in my notebook, and sometimes omega,
sometimes parenthesis, steps off the lengths of
these lines, and is strong as the guffaw
I woke myself with one night, for no reason
I could find on either side of sleep.